FACT? FICTION?

Ethan Allen and the Green Mountain Boys

Audrey Ades

Mitchell Lane
PUBLISHERS
2001 SW 31st Avenue
Hallandale, FL 33009
www.mitchelllane.com

Mitchell Lane
PUBLISHERS

Printing   1   2   3   4   5   6   7   8

Audie Murphy
Buffalo Bill Cody
The Buffalo Soldiers
Davy Crockett
Ethan Allen and the Green Mountain Boys
Eliot Ness

Francis Marion
The Pony Express
Robin Hood
The Tuskegee Airmen
Wyatt Earp
Zorro

Library of Congress Cataloging-in-Publication Data
Names: Ades, Audrey, author.
Title: Ethan Allen and the Green Mountain Boys / by Audrey Ades.
Description: Hallandale, FL : Mitchell Lane Publishers, 2018. |
    Series: Fact or fiction? | Includes bibliographical references and index. |
    Audience: Age 8-11. | Audience: Grade 4 to 6.
Identifiers: LCCN 2017009127 | ISBN 9781612289526 (library bound)
Subjects: LCSH: Allen, Ethan, 1738–1789. | Soldiers—United States—Biography. |
    United States—History—Revolution, 1775-1783—Biography. |
    Vermont—History—Revolution, 1775-1783.
Classification: LCC E207.A4 G34 2017 | DDC 974.3/03092 [B] —dc23
LC record available at https://lccn.loc.gov/2017009127

eBook ISBN: 978-1-61228-953-3

CONTENTS

Words in **bold** throughout can be found in the Glossary.

Governor Benning Wentworth of New Hampshire sold large plots of land to settlers like Ethan Allen and the Green Mountain Boys. The New York courts later ruled this land didn't belong to New Hampshire and was never legally his to

Land, Liberty, and the Green Mountain Boys

The Green Mountains span the state of Vermont, majestically covering approximately 250 miles from the northern border of Massachusetts to Quebec, Canada. They are the state's most significant geological feature and even gave Vermont its name. French explorer Samuel de Champlain called them *Vert Monts* ("Green Mountains" in French) in 1647.

In the early-to-mid 1700s, before the **American Revolution**, much of the land around the Green Mountains was wild and unclaimed. Like all **territory** in the American **colonies**, this land belonged to King George III. King George ruled from his throne in England and appointed royal governors to make sure his orders were obeyed.

By the mid-1700s, farmland in much of New England was becoming relatively scarce. So in 1749, Benning Wentworth, the royal governor of New Hampshire, began selling large tracts of land in the Green Mountains area to investors. These tracts became known as the New Hampshire Grants. Each tract, or grant, was roughly six miles on a side. In turn, the investors sold smaller parcels of land within their grants to **settlers** who would make their homes there. One of these settlers was a young man named Ethan Allen.

Life in the New Hampshire Grants was generally peaceful until the mid-1760s, when the royal governor of New York declared that Wentworth had been illegally selling the land. He claimed it belonged to New York. People from New York tried to push the settlers in the Grants off their property. But these settlers had been working their land for years. Sometimes with little more than an axe and a rifle, they cleared the forests, planted crops, and hunted for food. In this cold and unforgiving land, they built their homes and raised their families. They were not about to give it to the **Yorkers**.

After years of dispute, New Hampshire and New York brought their complaints to court in June 1770. Allen traveled by horse to New York to witness the trial and defend his land and the land of his neighbors.

There was no radio or telephone to spread the news of the outcome of the trial. Instead, the day after the trial, a group of men gathered at the Catamount Tavern in Bennington. The town was named for Bennington Wentworth. It had been part of the governor's very first grant. Now the men anxiously waited for Allen to return. Each of them owned land in the New Hampshire Grants. Their livelihoods, their ability to feed their families, and years of backbreaking labor were at stake.

Allen finally rode up to the tavern and drew water for his horse. The men ran out to meet him.

One look at their friend's fiery eyes told them all they needed to know. The New York Supreme Court had ruled that the New Hampshire Grants were illegal. To stay on their land, the settlers would have to pay a large fee to New York.

Allen told the men that the trial had been unfair. For example, the judge in the case, Robert Livingston, was himself a New Yorker with more than 160,000 acres to lose if he had ruled in favor of the New Hampshire Grants owners. Allen also said that the prosecutor had offered him money to quiet the settlers back home. Rejecting this bribe, Allen reportedly said, "The gods of the valleys [meaning New York] are not the gods of the hills [referring to the Green Mountains]."[1] If they didn't know what he meant by that, he dared them to come to Bennington and find out!

Enraged by what they heard, the men decided to form a local militia, a sort of informal army. They called themselves the Green Mountain Boys.

The Green Mountain Boys were not "boys" at all. They were rugged frontiersmen, farmers, and hunters who had risked everything for their land and their freedom. Among the original members were Allen's brothers Ira, Heman, and Levi, and his cousins Seth Warner and Remember Baker.

Armed with **muskets** and rifles, the Green Mountain Boys pledged not to allow the Yorkers to tax or **evict** settlers who had land grants from New Hampshire. They chose Allen as their leader. Standing six feet tall, strong as a bull, with a sharp mind and a

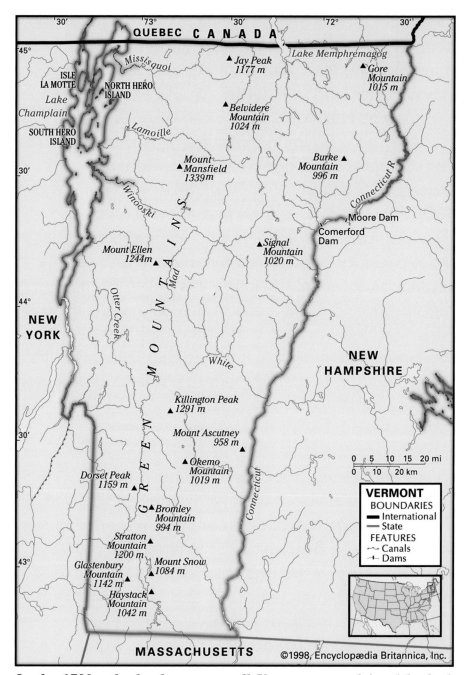

In the 1700s, the land we now call Vermont was claimed by both New York and New Hampshire. Maps of the time were crude and land boundaries were vague. Vermont declared itself an independent republic in 1777 and was accepted as the 14th state in 1791.

quick tongue, he inspired confidence and loyalty among his fellow landholders. In Allen, they had a trusted leader who cared deeply about their shared cause.

The Boys used threats, unofficial arrests, and intimidation to "persuade" many Yorkers to leave the New Hampshire settlers alone. But the first big test of their strength and organization as a militia came the following summer.

James Breakenridge was a Grant owner in Bennington. He had been tipped off that the Yorkers were coming to take his land and called upon the Green Mountain Boys for help. On July 1, 1771, 300 Yorkers and the sheriff of Albany, New York stormed Breakenridge's property. They intended to evict him and his family. As soon as the sheriff raised his axe to break down the door, 100 guns pointed directly at his head. Legend goes that although the sheriff commanded his troops to proceed into town, "the Yorkers stampeded for home."[2]

Any doubt about the effectiveness of the Green Mountain Boys disappeared on that hot July afternoon. The Boys, or the "Bennington Mob" as they were called by New York's governor, were so successful that a large reward was promised for Allen's arrest.

Ethan Allen's reputation as a defender of settlers' rights and independence quickly spread throughout the colonies. It wouldn't be long before the Green Mountain Boys would find even bigger ways to defend their freedom.

TICONDEROGA

This statue marks the burial spot of Ethan Allen in the Green Mount Cemetery in Burlington, Vermont. The figure of Allen is eight feet tall and carved from Vermont granite. It depicts him demanding the surrender of Fort Ticonderoga.

CHAPTER 2

Ethan: Strong and Solid

Historians do not agree on the year Ethan Allen was born. Was it 1737? 1738? Or 1739? Most sources agree that the date of his birth was January 21, although two biographers from the late 1800s state with certainty that he was born on January 10th.[1] What is clear is that he was the eldest of eight children born to Mary and Joseph Allen. When Allen was a small boy, his family moved from his birthplace of Litchfield, Connecticut to Cornwall, Connecticut, a small village with few other families.

The name Ethan comes from the Bible and means "strong and solid." Even as a child, Allen lived up to his name. Like all settler children, he worked hard. Just about everything the family had, they made themselves. Everything they ate, they either grew or hunted. Legend has it Allen could run a deer to the point of exhaustion and then catch it when it collapsed.[2]

Although there were no schools in Cornwall, Allen learned to read at an early age. Like most other settlers, Allen's simple home didn't have many books. But after the wood was chopped and the crops were

Ethan Allen was born in this house in Litchfield, Connecticut and lived here until his family moved to Cornwall in 1740. The house has been remodeled and expanded and is still lived in today.

planted, he read the Bible and anything else he could get his hands on.

Some members of his father's family had gone to college to become ministers. Joseph Allen thought the ministry would be a fitting profession for his eldest son as well. At age 17, Allen went to live with the Reverend Jonathon Lee, a relative who would prepare him to attend Yale College and become a minister. But just before he was about to start school, his father died. Suddenly the man of the family, Allen returned to the farm to help support his mother and seven siblings.

Farm life did not suit Allen. He craved action and adventure. Two years later, in 1757, a local militia unit fighting on the side of England in the French and

Indian War passed through Cornwall. Without hesitation, Allen joined them.

Allen didn't see much combat but his duty took him into the unsettled areas of the Green Mountains. The wild splendor of the land captured the young soldier's imagination. Even as he returned home, Allen planned to someday buy land there and raise a family.

In 1762, Allen married Mary Brownson. But the couple was not happy. Mary was **illiterate** and much stricter in her religious beliefs than her husband.

Allen also did not get along with some of his neighbors. In one case, a neighbor's pig wandered onto Allen's land. He caught the poor animal and served it to his family for supper.[3]

Allen felt suffocated by life in a small town. He wanted to live freely according to his own rules and beliefs. For example, many New England ministers believed that diseases such as **smallpox** were the will of God and that humans should not try to prevent them. Allen disagreed. So one day he became one of the first colonists to be **inoculated**. Standing in front of a church, Allen's friend Dr. Thomas Young made a small scratch on Allen's arm and rubbed a bit of pus from a smallpox blister into his open skin. Performing the inoculation in front of a church was a clear **rebuke** of this religious teaching.[4]

He also longed for wide-open spaces. Eventually he bought land in the Grants, built a home for his family, and began a new chapter of his life.

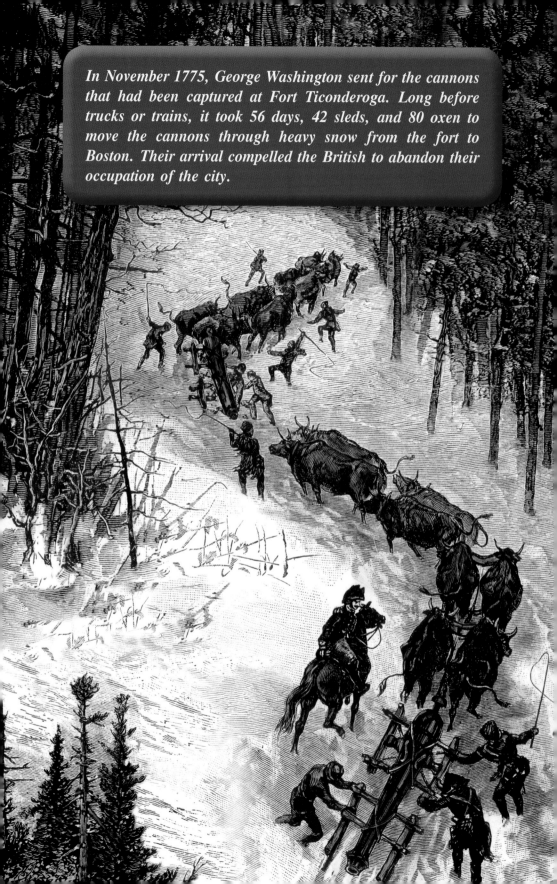

In November 1775, George Washington sent for the cannons that had been captured at Fort Ticonderoga. Long before trucks or trains, it took 56 days, 42 sleds, and 80 oxen to move the cannons through heavy snow from the fort to Boston. Their arrival compelled the British to abandon their occupation of the city.

War

Between 1770 and 1775, Allen often rode with the Green Mountain Boys, successfully defending their lands. More than 1,000 Green Mountain frontiersmen would eventually join Allen's command.[1] He also wrote and published pamphlets, railing against the royal governors who acted on behalf of King George and raising public sympathy for the hard-working settlers.

But trouble was brewing in the lower colonies.

In late April, 1775, a weary horseman from Massachusetts burst through the doors of the Catamount Tavern. He was looking for Ethan Allen. Allen's reputation as a defender of liberty and freedom for the common man was well known among the **patriot** leaders. The messenger shoved a crumpled message into Allen's large hand. On April 19, British soldiers had fired shots at patriots on Lexington Green just outside of Boston. As the day wore on, the patriots fired back. The Revolutionary War had begun. Years later, Allen wrote that the British attack at Lexington "thoroughly electrified my mind and fully determined me to take part with my country."[2]

Allen had long since given up his loyalty to King George. Years of unfair taxes and fees had turned many **colonists** against Mother England. Shortly after Lexington, the **Continental Congress** in Philadelphia began debating whether or not to break away from English rule and establish a new and independent country.

Allen had high hopes of making a name for himself. He quickly seized upon a way that he and his men could help the **rebel** army in their fight for freedom.

Fort Ticonderoga lay at the southern end of Lake Champlain. It was near an area of the New Hampshire Grants that Allen knew well. This British fort was believed to have a large reserve of firearms and cannons. Allen knew that this artillery would be useful in the war for independence. Equally important, if the Americans had control of the fort, they could stop the British from attacking the New England colonies by coming down through Canada.

Historians disagree about the next part of the story. Allen later wrote, "directions were privately sent to me from the then colony (now state) of Connecticut, to raise the Green Mountain Boys (and if possible) with them to surprise and take the fortress Ticonderoga."[3]

Other accounts suggest that Allen sent his brother Heman to the patriot leaders in Hartford, requesting permission to execute his plan. This version says that after riding hard for a week, Heman returned with the permission his brother had sought.[4]

Allen sent a spy to the fort. He learned that the walls were in poor condition, it was lightly guarded, and the gunpowder was wet and unusable. Confident he could conquer Fort Ticonderoga, he set the date for the attack: May 10, 1775, before dawn's first light.

A day or two before the attack, Allen gathered about 130 Green Mountain Boys on the shores of Lake Champlain. Allen had hoped to have twice that number to charge the fort but it was planting season. The last two seasons had been dry and lean and many farmers simply could not leave their land and risk losing their future crops. Dressed in home-sewn coats, **tunics**, and moccasins, Allen realized that his "soldiers" were really just an untrained company of brave hunters, farmers, store clerks, and free African-American men ready to lay down their lives in the name of freedom.

Fort Ticonderoga lay just across Lake Champlain, about a mile from where the Boys were camped. He sent his Boys to borrow or steal the boats they needed to make the crossing. Ignoring his exhaustion and hunger, Allen squinted across the bleak horizon. The last thing he expected to see was a short little man in a scarlet red uniform.

"With my sword drawn over my head, I demanded an immediate surrender of the garrison, to which he (Captain William Delaplace) complied," Allen wrote in his auto-biography describing the victory at Fort Ticonderoga.

Fort Ticonderoga and a Visitor

I n the 18th century, communication between the colonies was slow and unreliable. The rebel leaders in Massachusetts didn't know that Connecticut had given Allen permission to attack the fort. So they gave Benedict Arnold, a New England smuggler and up-and-coming patriot leader (and eventual traitor), the authority to assemble a band of volunteer soldiers to attack Fort Ticonderoga.

Exactly when and where the two men met may be lost to history. Many accounts say Arnold arrived with 60 militiamen from Connecticut and Massachusetts, while others maintain that he "brought nothing to the fight but himself."[1]

Bossy and self-important, Arnold demanded that Allen step aside and allow him to lead the attack. But the Green Mountain Boys refused to follow his command. Realizing he had no choice, Arnold ultimately agreed to let Allen lead the troops. To soothe the tension between them, Allen proposed they co-lead the attack.

By nightfall, the men had found only two boats. Sunrise was just a few hours away and only Allen, Arnold, and 83 men were in position to carry out their mission. Allen and Arnold faced a terrible decision. Should they attack according to plan before dawn or postpone it and wait for more men to arrive? They decided to launch the assault.

The two commanders and their men charged the south gate of Fort Ticonderoga. The sole guard, caught completely by surprise, abandoned his post without a fight. Entering the barracks, the men easily overwhelmed the sleepy British soldiers and took their weapons.

Next, Allen found his way to the quarters of commanding officer Captain William Delaplace and pounded on the door. "In the name of the Great **Jehovah** and the Continental Congress"[2] he demanded that Delaplace surrender the fort. Delaplace was stunned—he didn't even know the war had begun! Still in his nightwear, Delaplace had no choice but to hand his sword over to Allen and surrender the fort.

The battle at Ticonderoga secured a **strategic** fort on the northern border and captured 43 cannons and 16 **mortars**. The cannons were hauled over the Adirondack Mountains and used by the patriots to drive the British out of Boston in the following March.

Much has been written about what really occurred between Ethan Allen and Benedict Arnold on the morning of May 10th. Although the popular story says that Allen and Arnold co-led the attack, many historians find it hard to believe that Allen would have let Arnold share the glory. Some sources report that Allen led the attack once the men were past the front gate and that he alone confronted Delaplace at the door of his quarters. Certainly that's how Allen remembered it. In his 1779 **autobiography**, he makes no mention of Arnold's role in the attack at all.

Allen's memory might have misled him into thinking he had made his surrender demand to Captain Delaplace, whereas most accounts indicate it was to a junior officer instead.[3] He may also have exaggerated when he claimed the capture of "about 100 pieces of cannon, one 13 inch mortar and several swivels,"[4]—about twice the amount as other sources report. Further, whereas Allen wrote that he had used lofty language invoking Jehovah and the Continental Congress when he banged on the captain's door, one of his men said he shouted, "Come out of there, you old rat!" and peppered his demand with a few profanities.[5]

Although the myth persists that the fall of Fort Ticonderoga was due to Allen's great military skill, the facts seem to indicate that it was due more to the lack of preparation by the British.[6] The famous Battle of Ticonderoga was hardly a battle at all. No shots were fired and only two men were slightly injured. Still, news of this first victory for the patriots made Ethan Allen an instant hero.

This painting probably does not show what really happened at the capture of Fort Ticonderoga. By all accounts, there was no fighting between the Green Mountain Boys and the British soldiers, most of whom were asleep and completely unprepared for the attack.

CHAPTER 5

The Fight for Independence Continues

In the days after their victory at Fort Ticonderoga, the Green Mountain Boys and Arnold's men attacked and captured nearby Fort Crown Point, Fort George, Fort Saint-Jean, and the largest British ship on Lake Champlain, the HMS *Royal George*.

Although these victories were good news for the rebel army, Congress was not happy that Allen and Arnold had acted without its permission. Concerned that Allen was getting too big for his **britches**, they did not make him an officer of the army as he had hoped and expected. To add to Allen's disappointment, the Green Mountain Boys soon elected his cousin, Seth Warner, as their new leader. Perhaps even Allen's loyal followers had grown weary of his headstrong behaviors and habit of charging ahead without securing the proper equipment, food, or protection for his men.[1]

A few months later, Allen decided to prove his worth to the patriot cause by attacking Montreal, Canada. He believed many Canadians could be convinced to support the Americans in their fight against the British. His friend, John Brown, agreed to follow Allen's men with more soldiers if they needed help.

Just before dawn on September 24, with only 100 men at his side, Allen tried to storm the gates of Montreal. But the British citizens of the city who were still loyal to the king had been warned about Allen's plan. Over 300 British, Canadian, and Native American troops charged his men at the city gates.[2] Brown's troops never arrived.

Most of Allen's men ran off in fear. The ones who remained fought valiantly for over two hours before Allen realized that if he didn't surrender, they would likely die. He later wrote, "I then saluted [the Canadian commander] with my tongue in a harsh manner, and told him . . . I would surrender, provided I could be treated with honor."[3] The commander agreed.

Allen endured harsh punishments and conditions he would hardly call "honorable" in British jails and prison ships for more than a year. In November 1776, he was transferred back to New York. Still angry about his **captivity**, he refused to obey the rules of his **parole** and landed back in jail for another eight months.

In 1779, Allen published his autobiography, *A Narrative of Col. Ethan Allen's Captivity, Written by Himself*. It detailed his victory at Fort Ticonderoga and the cruel treatment he suffered in prison. The book became a best seller. It was reprinted 60 times and remained in print for over 200 years.[4]

During Allen's imprisonment, the area around the Green Mountains had declared its independence as the Vermont Republic. But it had not been accepted into the union by Congress. Frustrated by the situation, Allen ventured one last risk on behalf of his beloved land.

Acting without orders or permission, he tried to convince England to allow Vermont to become an independent state within the British Empire. These discussions, called the Haldimand Negotiations, lasted from 1781 to 1784. It is unlikely that Allen seriously wanted Vermont to belong to England. Most historians believe he was trying to pressure Congress to include Vermont in the new United States.[5]

During this time, Allen reunited with his family. His work and his imprisonment had kept him away from his wife and five children for several years. He learned that his eldest son, Joe, had died of smallpox. Some sources say Allen suffered from depression and drank too much as he struggled to cope with this loss of his son.[6] Not long afterward, his wife Mary also died. Allen soon married Frances Buchanan and had three more children with her.

Allen spent his last years on his farm in Burlington. He continued to write pamphlets and letters in support of Vermont's acceptance into the United States. On a cold winter day in February, 1789, Allen suffered a stroke or a heart attack and died the next day. He had just turned 51.

Two years later, on March 4, 1791, Vermont joined the Union as the country's 14th state.

FACT OR FICTION?

Ethan Allen was an American folk hero even before he died. He is considered the Father of Vermont independence and June 23rd is officially Ethan Allen Day. Statues of Allen stand in Burlington, Allen's home when he died, and in Rutland, the state capital. Rutland and Bennington (home of the original Catamount Tavern) have statues commemorating the Green Mountain Boys. Over two centuries after the Battle of Ticonderoga, the Vermont Army National Guard and Air National Guard still refer to themselves as the Green Mountain Boys.

History books are full of **contradictory** portraits of Allen. Some paint him as a boastful, **willful** man whose primary leadership qualities were self-exaggeration, threats, and bluffs. Others focus on his indisputable bravery and commitment to the freedom and liberty of the common man. What is surely true is that Allen was a patriot who seemed to know no fear.

Perhaps most important, Ethan Allen lived the concepts of individual liberty that represented the spirit of the Revolutionary period. His risk-all attitudes and behavior caught the imagination of a people ready to

Fort Ticonderoga is now a military museum where visitors can learn about the fort's construction, weapons, and role in the American Revolution.

break away from the rule of an oppressive king and begin a nation of their own.

   Today, we are still fascinated by this wild patriot who defended the rights of Vermont's early settlers, led the victorious Battle of Fort Ticonderoga, and provided the cannons that helped the colonists expel the British from the city of Boston. Like the giant statues that stand in his honor, his legacy as a hero of Vermont and the American Revolution is larger than life.

Chapter 1: Land, Liberty and the Green Mountain Boys
1. Henry Hall, *Ethan Allen: The Robin Hood of Vermont* (New York: D. Appleton and Company, 1895), p. 27.
2. Ibid., p. 28.

Chapter 2: Ethan: Strong and Solid
1. Henry Hall, *Ethan Allen: The Robin Hood of Vermont* (New York: D. Appleton and Company, 1895), p. 18; Grace Graylock Niles, *The Hoosac Valley: Its Legends and Its History* (New York and London: The Knickerbocker Press, 1912), p. 369.
2. Virginia Aronson, *Ethan Allen: Revolutionary Hero* (Philadelphia: Chelsea House, 2001), p. 19.
3. Janelle Pavao, "Ethan Allen." RevolutionaryWar.net. http://www.revolutionary-war.net/ethan-allen.html
4. Cindy Jacobs, "Great Moments in Freethought: Allen's Inoculation." Patheos.com. http://www.patheos.com/blogs/unreasonablefaith/2011/09/great-moments-in-freethough-allens-inoculation/

Chapter 3: War
1 Stephen C. Arch, editor, *A Narrative of Colonel Ethan Allen's Captivity* (Acton, MA: Copley Publishing Group, 2000), p. viii.
2. Ibid., p. 5.
3. Ibid.
4. Willard Sterne Randall, *Ethan Allen, His Life and Times* (New York: W.W. Norton, 2011), p. 26.

Chapter 4: Fort Ticonderoga and a Visitor
1. Michael Schellhammer, "The Legacy of Ethan Allen." *Journal of the American Revolution*, March 11, 2013. https://allthingsliberty.com/2013/03/the-legacy-of-ethan-allen/
2. Stephen C. Arch, editor, *A Narrative of Colonel Ethan Allen's Captivity* (Acton, MA: Copley Publishing Group, 2000), p. 7.
3. Kennedy Hickman, "American Revolution: Capture of Fort Ticonderoga." Thoughtco.com. https://www.thoughtco.com/capture-of-fort-ticonderoga-2360180
4. Arch, *Narrative*, p. 7.
5. Willard Sterne Randall, *Ethan Allen, His Life and Times* (New York: W.W. Norton, 2011), p. 309.
6. "Who Was Ethan Allen?" Ethan Allen Homestead Museum. http://www.Ethanallenhomestead.org/education.html

Chapter 5: The Fight for Independence Continues
1. Martin Kelly, "Ethan Allen: Revolutionary War Hero." Thoughtco. https://www.thoughtco.com/ethan-allen-revolutionary-war-hero-4054307
2. Willard Sterne Randall, *Ethan Allen, His Life and Times* (New York: W.W. Norton, 2011), pp. 372-374.
3. Stephen C. Arch, editor, *A Narrative of Colonel Ethan Allen's Captivity* (Acton, MA: Copley Publishing Group, 2000), p. 14.
4. Randall, *Ethan Allen*, p. xi.
5. Michael Bellesiles, "Ethan Allen," *American National Biography*, Vol. 1 (New York, Oxford University Press, 1999), p. 310.
6. Michael Schellhammer, "The Legacy of Ethan Allen." *Journal of the American Revolution*, March 11, 2013. https://allthingsliberty.com/2013/03/the-legacy-of-ethan-allen/

American Colonies (uh-MER-uh-kuhn KAHL-uh-neez)–a group of 13 British-owned territories on the east coast of North America

American Revolution (uh-MER-e-kuhn rev-e-lLOO-shen)–a war between the American colonies and Great Britain that took place between 1775 and 1783.

autobiography (aw-toe-bi-AWG-ruh-fee)–a biography written by the person it is about

britches (BRICH-ez)–another word for pants

captivity (kap-TIV-uh-tee)–time spent in prison or not free

colonists (KAHL-uh-nests)–people who live in a colony

Continental Congress (kawn-tin-EN-tuhl CAHNG-gress)–representatives from the 13 colonies who met in Philadelphia from 1774-1781

contradictory (kawn-truh-DIK-tuh-ree)–something that is the opposite of what someone has said

evict (ee-VICT)–to put a person out of a property

illiterate (il-LIT-uh-ruht)–unable to read; having little or no education

inoculated (in-AWK-yu-lay-tuhd)–introduced a substance into a body to protect against or treat a disease

Jehovah (ji-HO-vuh)–another word for God

legacy (LEG-e-see)–something left by a person

mortars (MOHR-tehrz)–short cannons used to fire shells at low speed and high angles

muskets (MUSS-kets)–firearms used before rifles

parole (puh-ROHL)–early release of a prisoner

patriot (PAY-tree-uht)–a person who loves his or her country

rebel (REB-ull)–a person who refuses to give in to authority

rebuke (ree-BYOOK)–sharp disapproval or criticism

settlers (SET-luhrz)–people who establish a home and develop the land in a new region

smallpox (SMAWL-poks)–a sometimes deadly disease caused by a virus

strategic (stra-TEE-jik)–part of a planned project

tunics (TYU-niks)–shirts or jackets reaching just below the hips, sometimes tied with a belt

willful (WIL-ful)–stubborn

Yorkers (YOERK-ers)–a name for people from New York

"About Colonel Ethan Allen." Ethan Allen.org. http://www. ethanallen.org/html/about_col_allen.html

Allen, Ethan. *Reason: The Only Oracle of Man, A Compendious System of Natural Religion*. Boston: J.P. Mendum, Cornhill, 1854.

"American Revolution: Capture of Fort Ticonderoga." Thoughtco.com. https://www.thoughtco.com/capture-of-fort-ticonderoga-2360180

Arch, Stephen, editor. *A Narrative of Colonel Ethan Allen's Captivity*. Acton, MA: Copley Publishing Group, 2000.

Aronson, Virginia. *Ethan Allen: Revolutionary Hero*. Philadelphia: Chelsea House Publishers, 2001.

Bellesiles, Michael. *American National Biography*, Vol. 1. New York: Oxford University Press, 1999.

"Ethan Allen." Encyclopedia.com. http://www.encyclopedia.com/ people/history/us-history-biographies/ethan-allen

"Ethan Allen Biography." Biography.com. http://www.biography. com/people/ethan-allen-9181414

"Ethan Allen Captures Fort Ticonderoga, 1775." EyeWitness to History.com. http://www.eyewitnesstohistory.com/ethanallen.html

"Ethan Allen Day." Ethan Allen Homestead.org. http://www. ethanallenhomestead.org/ethanallenday.html.

"Ethan Allen is born." History.com. http://www.history.com/this-day-in-history/ethan-allen-is-born

Hall, Henry. *Ethan Allen: The Robin Hood of Vermont*. New York: D. Appleton and Company, 1895.

"Intelligence Throughout History: The Capture of Fort Ticonderoga, 1775." CIA.gov. https://www.cia.gov/news-information/ featured-story-archive/2010-featured-story-archive/capture-of-fort-ticonderoga.html

Jacobs, Cindy. "Great Moments in Free Thought: Allen's Inoculation." Patheos.com. http://www.patheos.com/blogs/ unreasonablefaith/2011/09/great-moments-in-freethough-allens-inoculation/

Kelly, Martin. "Ethan Allen: Revolutionary War Hero." Thoughtco. com. https://www.thoughtco.com/ethan-allen-revolutionary-war-hero-4054307

Niles, Grace Graylock. *The Hoosac Valley: Its Legends and Its History*. New York and London: The Knickerbocker Press, 1912.

Pavao, Janelle. "Ethan Allen." RevolutionaryWar.net. http://www. revolutionary-war.net/ethan-allen.html

Randall, Willard Sterne. *Ethan Allen, His Life and Times*. New York: W.W. Norton, 2011.

Schellhammer, Michael. "The Legacy of Ethan Allen." *Journal of the American Revolution*. https://allthingsliberty.com/2013/03/the-legacy-of-ethan-allen/

"Who Was Ethan Allen?" Ethan Allen Homestead.org. http://www.ethanallenhomestead.org/education.html

FURTHER READING

Aronson, Virginia. *Ethan Allen: Revolutionary Hero*. Philadelphia: Chelsea House Publishers, 2001.

Hahn, Michael. *Ethan Allen: A Life of Adventure*. Shelburne, VT: New England Press, 1994.

Haugen, Brenda. *Ethan Allen: Green Mountain Rebel*. Minneapolis, MN: Compass Point Books, 2005.

Hossell, Karen. *Ethan Allen* (American War Biographies). Chicago: Heinemann Library, 2004.

Raabe, Emily. *Ethan Allen: The Green Mountain Boys, and Vermont's Path to Statehood*. New York: Rosen, 2002.

ON THE INTERNET

American Revolution, Patriots and Loyalists
http://www.ducksters.com/history/american_revolution/patriots_and_loyalists.php

Ethan Allen
http://theamericanrevolution.org/peopleDetail.aspx?people=23

Ethan Allen Biography for Kids
http://mrnussbaum.com/ethan-allen-biography-for-kids/

Green Mountain Boys Flag
http://mrnussbaum.com/green-mountain-boys-flag/

ABOUT THE AUTHOR

As an adult, Audrey Ades developed a love for history and now wishes she had paid more attention in school. These days, she reads lots of history books and has written several about people who have left their marks on the world in quiet but important ways. She has been published by Chicken Soup for the Soul, Schoolwide, and Bumples Magazine. Audrey lives in Florida with her husband and son, who both know a lot about history, and her Pomeranian, Cookie, who doesn't seem to know much at all.